BAD
KITTIES

Celebrating good times and bad behavior

© 2005 Willow Creek Press

Published by Willow Creek Press, P.O. Box 147, Minocqua, Wisconsin 54548

Design: Donnie Rubo

Printed in Canada

© Renee Stockdale/AnimalsAnimals

Speak when you
are **angry**
and you will
make the best
speech you will
ever **regret.**

- Ambrose

Most people

want to be

delivered from

temptation

but would

like it to

stay in touch.

- Robert Orban

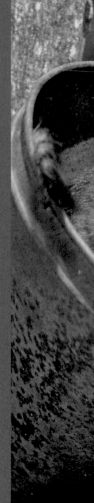

But pleasures

are like poppies spread;
You seize the flower, its
bloom is shed.

- Robert Burns

Women keep

a special corner

of their hearts

for **sins** they

never committed.

- Cornelia Otis

Guilt is

God's way

of letting

you know

that you're

having too

good a time.

- Dave Barry

What makes resisting

temptation

difficult for many people

is they don't want to

discourage it completely.

- Franklin P. Jones

Sin with the multitude
and your **guilt**
is as great as if you alone
had done the wrong.

- Tryon

Nothing sharpens

sight like

envy.

- Thomas Fuller

Anger

is natural.
You just
have to
learn to
hang out
with it.

- Tori Amos

If you

do not

want the

fruits

of sin

stay out of

the devils

orchard.

- Unknown

The greatest
incitement
to guilt
is the hope
of sinning
with impunity.

- *Cicero*

Some rise
by **sin,**

and some by
virtue fall.

- Shakespeare

I have a right to my **anger,** and
I don't want anyone telling me I
shouldn't be, that it's not nice to be,
and that something's wrong with
me because I get **angry.**

- Maxine Waters

The best years of your life are the ones in which **you** decide your problems are your own. You do not blame them on your mother, the ecology, or the president. **You** realize that you control your own destiny.

- Albert Ellis

He that but looketh on a plate of ham and eggs to lust after it hath already committed breakfast in his heart.

- C.S.Lewis

No animal ever invented

anything so bad as
drunkenness –
or so good as drink

- Lord Chesterton

The only thing wrong with

doing nothing is

that you never know when

you're finished.

- Unknown

Ellen Liman
with Lewis Liman

MADE WITH OAK

FRIEDMAN-WEISS / WISE

The Collecting Book

ISBN 0 14
00.52682

Guilt is
the price we pay
willingly for doing
what we are going
to do anyway.

- Isabelle Holland

People who

fly into a

rage

always make

a bad landing.

- Will Rogers

There two types of people in
this world, good and **bad.**
The good sleep better, but the
bad seem to enjoy the
waking hours much more.

- Woody Allen

Take your life in

your own hands,

and what happens?

A terrible thing:

no one to

blame.

- Erica Jong

There two types of people in this world, good and **bad.** The good sleep better, but the **bad** seem to enjoy the waking hours much more.

- Woody Allen

Take your life in

your own hands,

and what happens?

A terrible thing:

no one to

blame.

- Erica Jong

The trouble

with resisting

temptation

is it may

never come

your way again.

- Korman's Law

Every normal person
must be **tempted**
at times to spit upon their
hands, hoist the black flag,
and begin slitting throats.

- Lucanus

Fighting

is essentially

a masculine thing;

a woman's weapon

is her tongue.

- Hermoine Gingold

© Norvia Behling

The **thorns** which I have reaped are of the tree I planted; they have **torn** me, and I bleed. I should have known what fruit would spring from such a seed.

- Lord Byron

© Sharon Eide/Elizabeth Flynn

There is a charm about the
forbidden that makes
it unspeakably desirable.

- *Mark Twain*

But, oh! What mighty
magician can assuage a
woman's envy?

- *Unknown*

If you know someone
who tries to drown
their **sorrows,**
you might tell
them **sorrows**
know how to swim.

- H. Jackson Brown, Jr

It is always easier to **fight** for one's principles than to live up to them.

- Alfred Adler

The only way to get rid of **temptation** is to yield to it.

- *Oscar Wilde*

Laziness

is nothing more

than the habit

of resting before

you get tired.

- Jules Renard

Guilt is
present in the
very hesitation,
even though
the deed not
be committed.

- *Cicero*

In certain trying circumstances, urgent circumstances, desperate circumstances, **profanity** furnishes a relief denied even to prayer.

- Mark Twain

The unforgivable crime is soft hitting.
Do not **hit** at all if it can be avoided;
but never hit softly.

- Theodore Roosevelt

All are tempted.
There is no one that lives
that can't be broken down,
provided it is the right
temptation put in the
right spot.

- Henry Ward Beecher

Without the spice of **guilt,** sin cannot be fully savored.

- Alexander Chase

It's all right letting yourself go, as long as you get **yourself** back.

- Mick Jagger

You will do **foolish** things, but do them with enthusiasm.

- *Colette*

The **sinning**
is the best
part of repentance.

- Arab proverb

I have a

tremendous

amount of

anger,

but I like to

save it – for my

loved ones.

- *Susan Sullivan*

I like the word
"indolence."

It makes my laziness

seem classy.

- *Bern Williams*

Those who flee

temptation

generally leave a

forwarding address.

- Lane Olinghouse

Calm self-confidence is as far from conceit as the desire to earn a decent living is remote from greed.

- *Channing Pollock*